Alef Bet Tracing and Practice

Tip:

You can get even more writing practice by creating reusable sheets!

1. Take this book apart.
   Rip off the cover to more easily tear out its pages.
2. Place individual sheets into sheet protectors.
3. Write on the sheets with dry-erase markers.
4. Wipe off the marker to reuse.

ISBN-13: 978-1-951462-04-8

אוהל

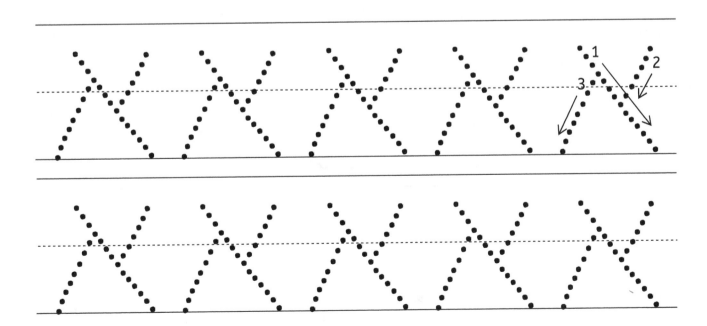

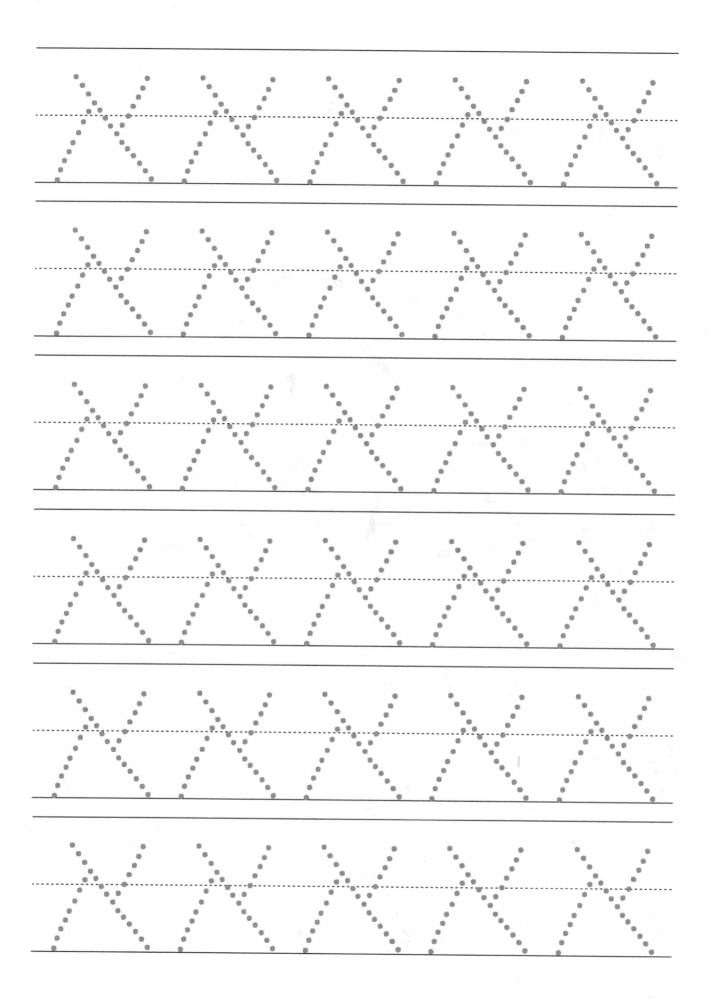

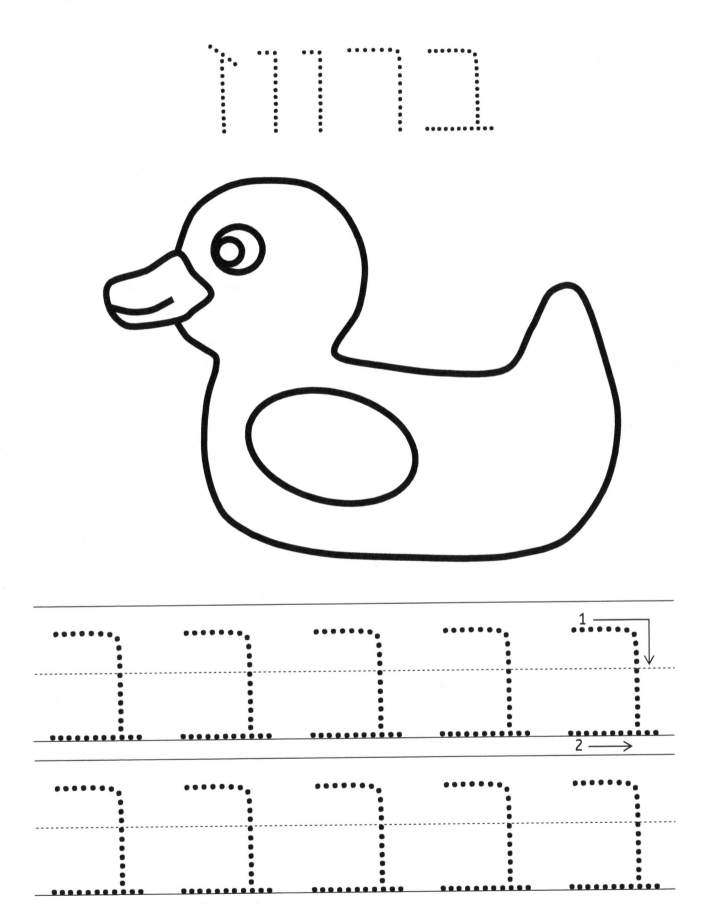

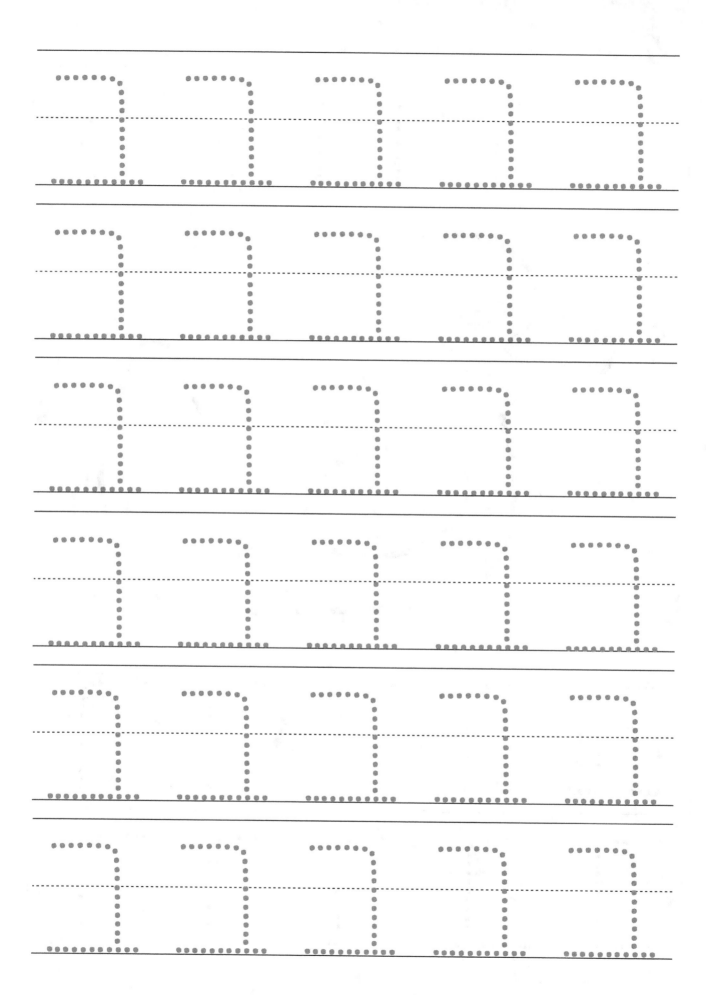

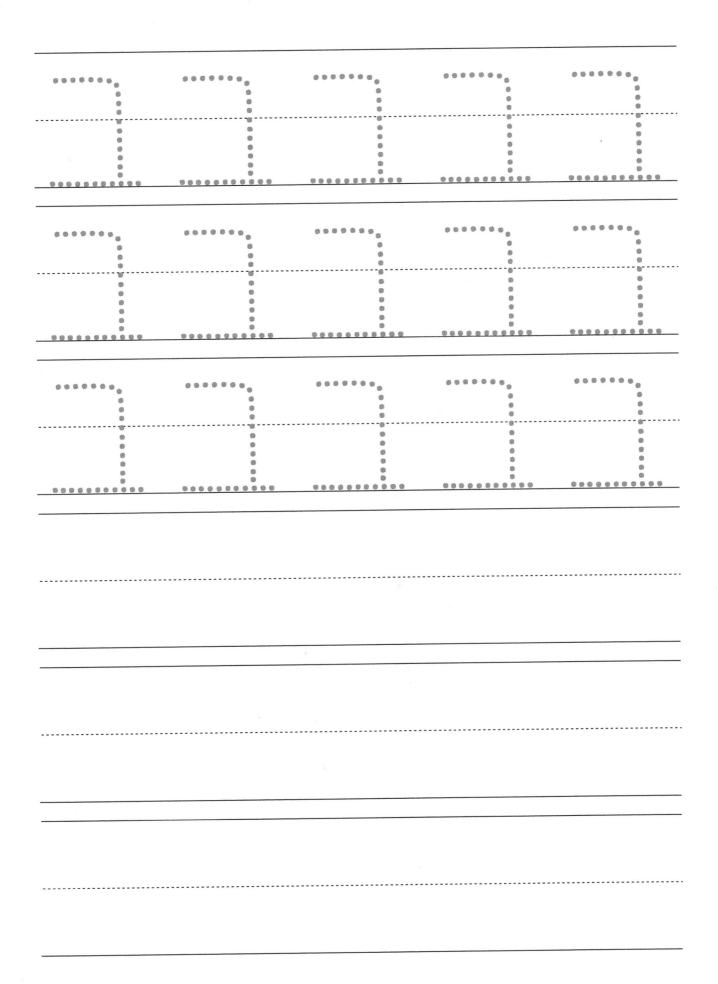

גיטרה

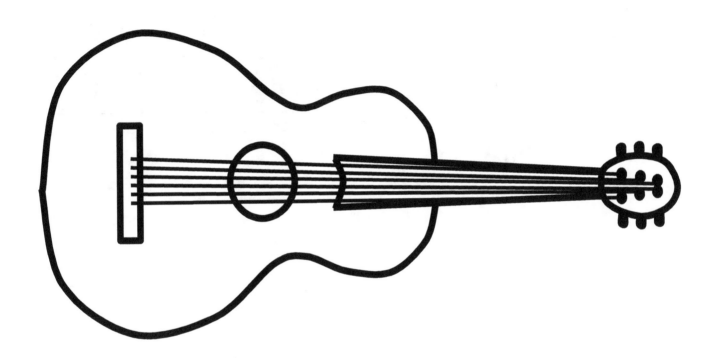

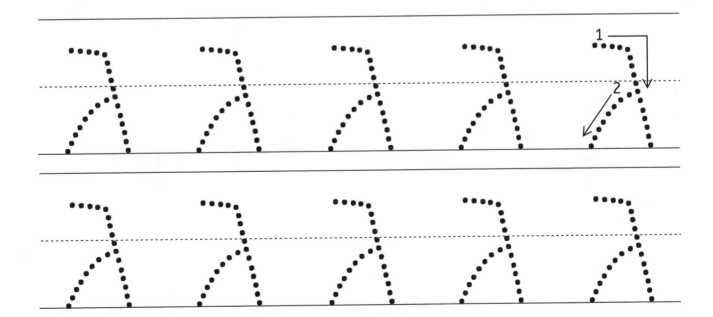

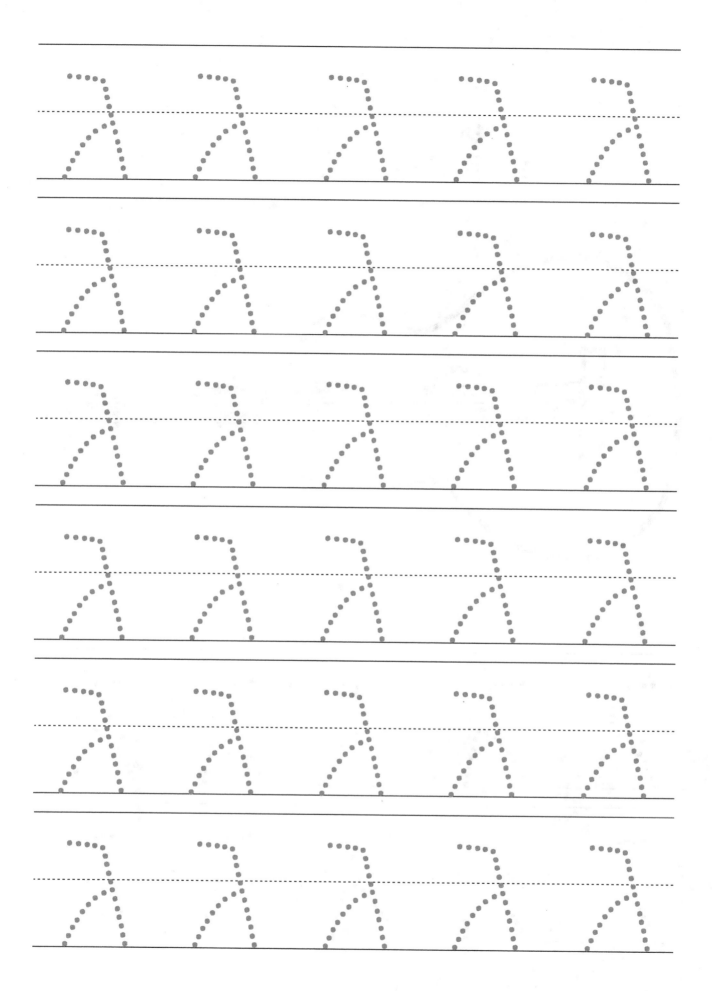

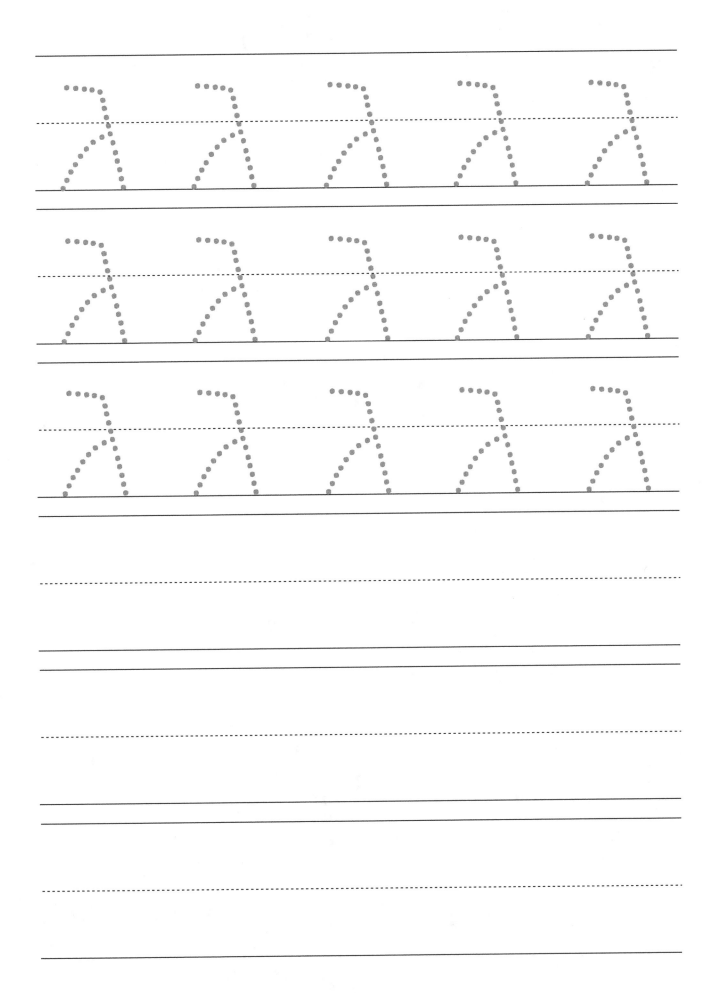

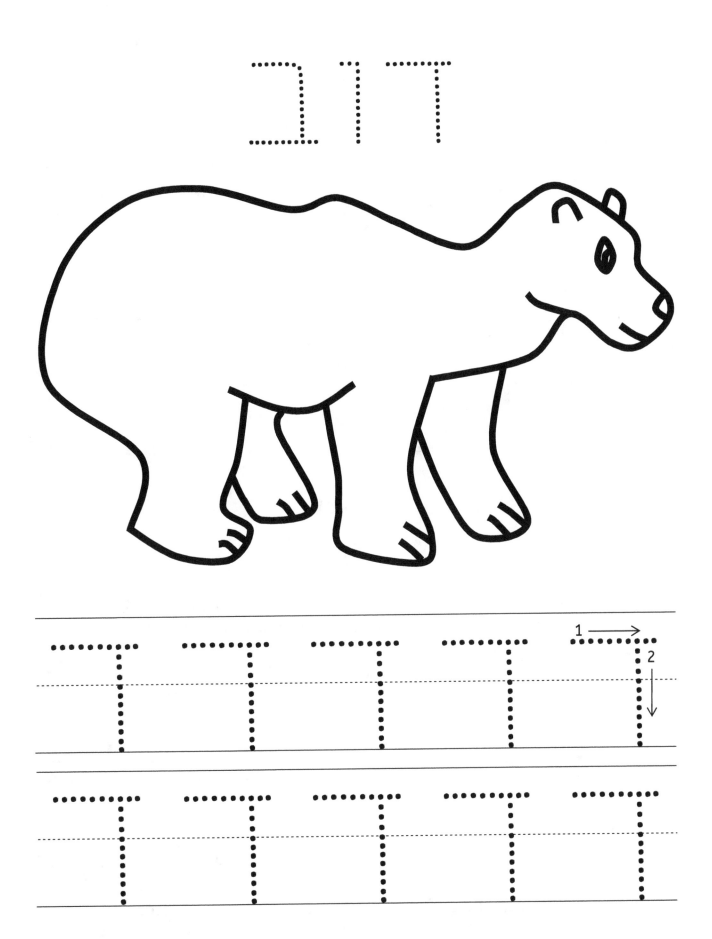

T T T T T

T T T T T

T T T T T

T T T T T

T T T T T

T T T T T

T T T T T

T T T T T

T T T T T

שמלה

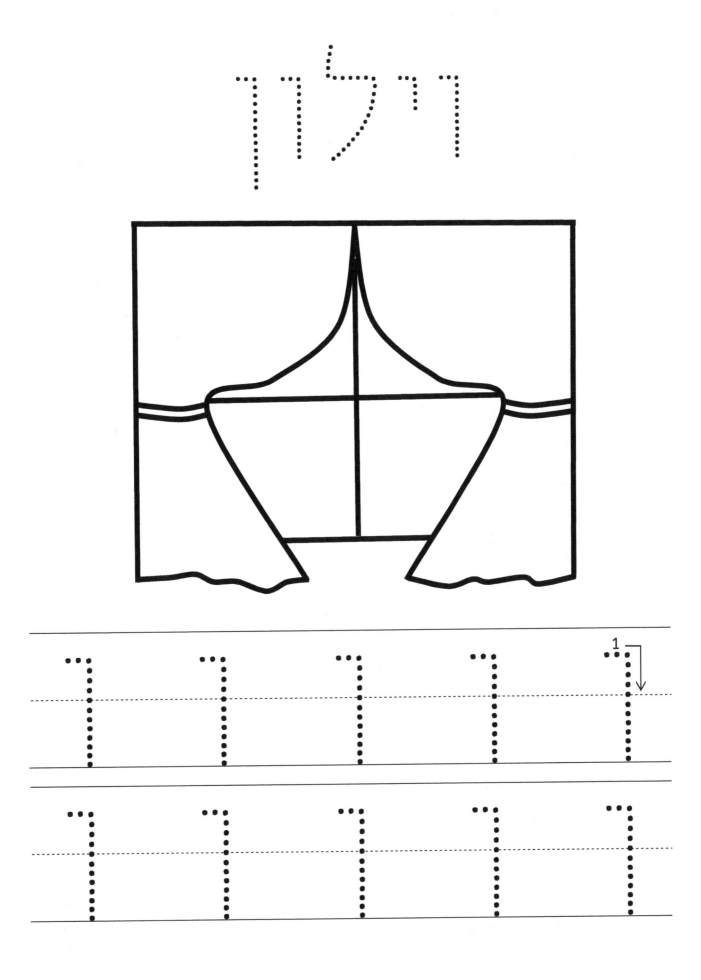

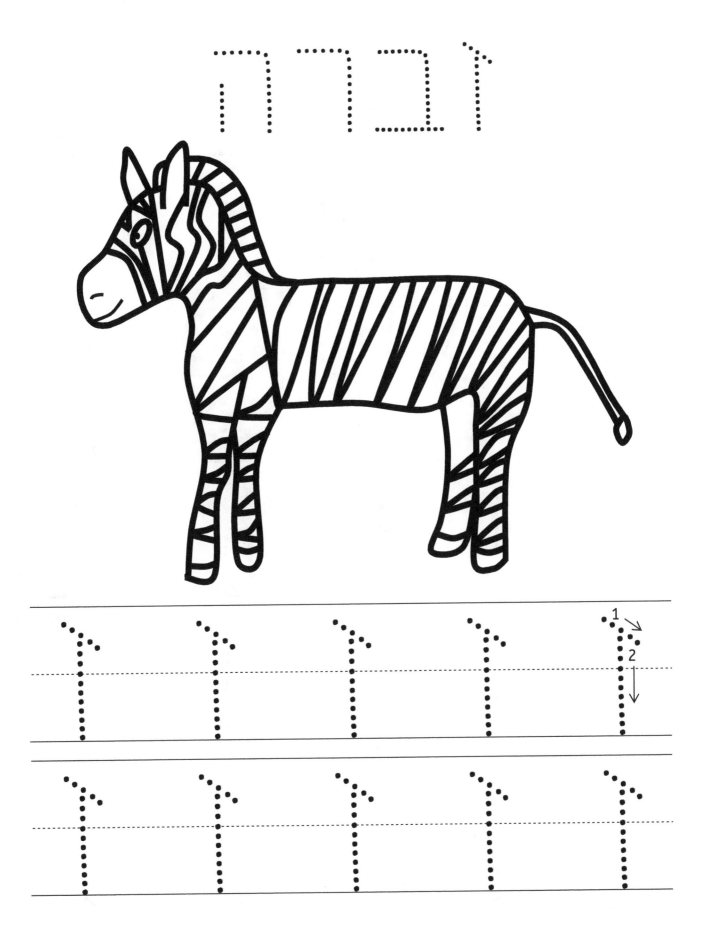

חלב

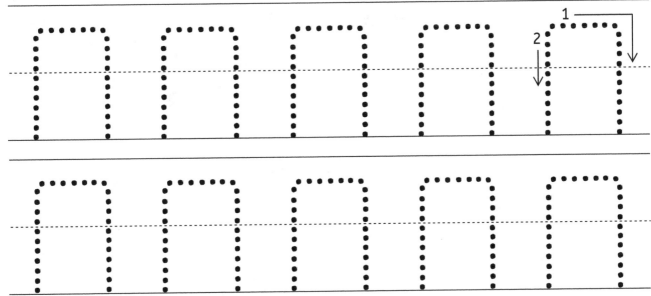

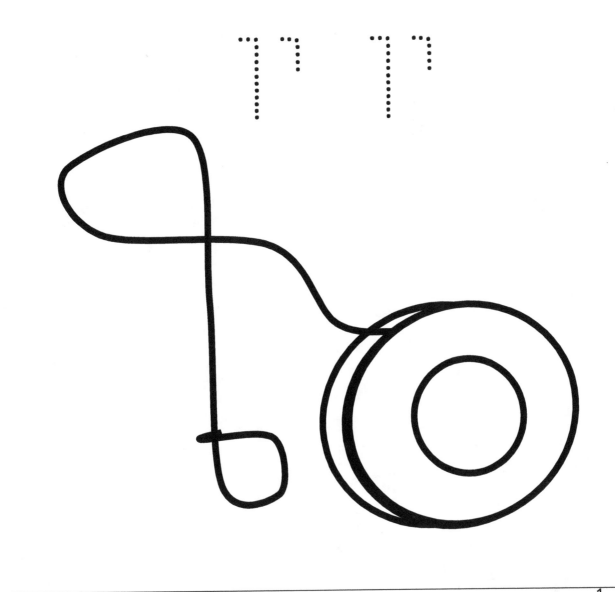

ㄱ   ㄱ   ㄱ   ㄱ   ㄱ

ㄱ   ㄱ   ㄱ   ㄱ   ㄱ

ㄱ   ㄱ   ㄱ   ㄱ   ㄱ

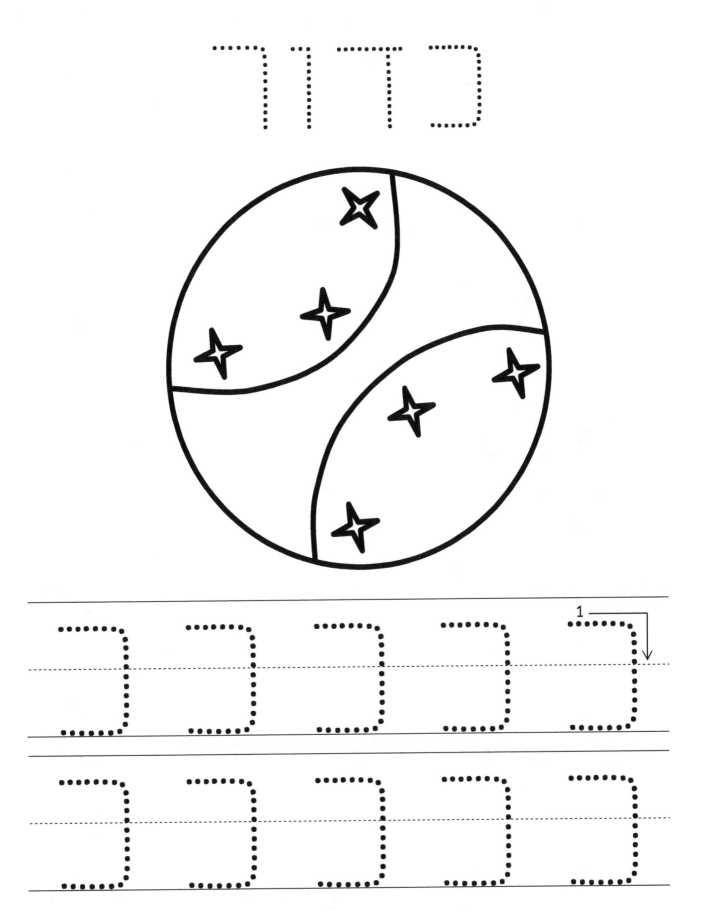

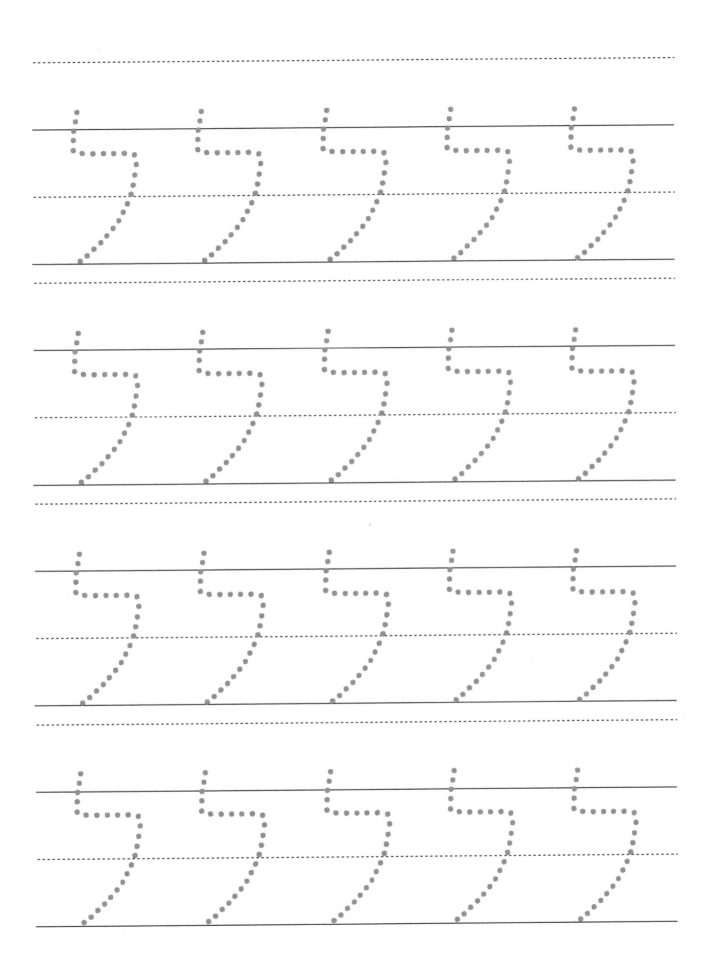

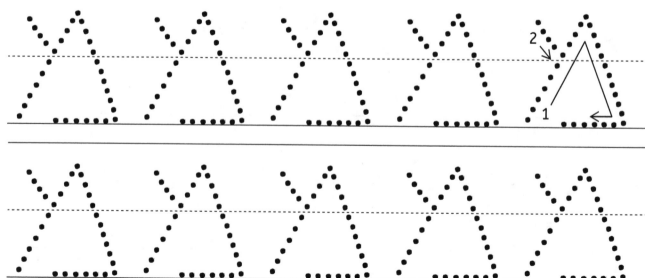

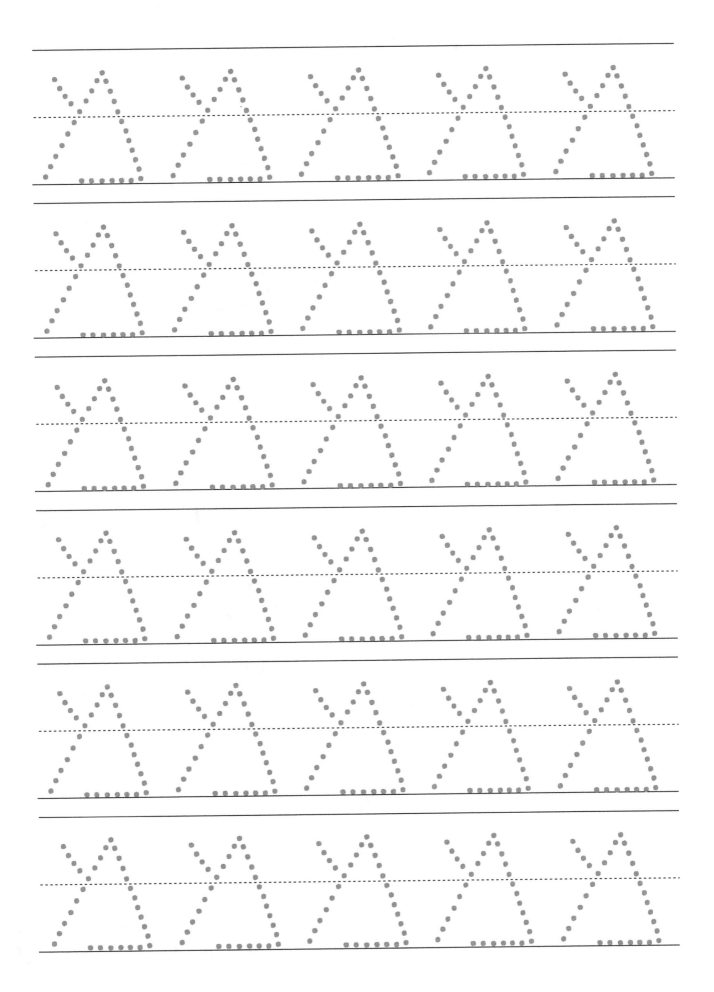

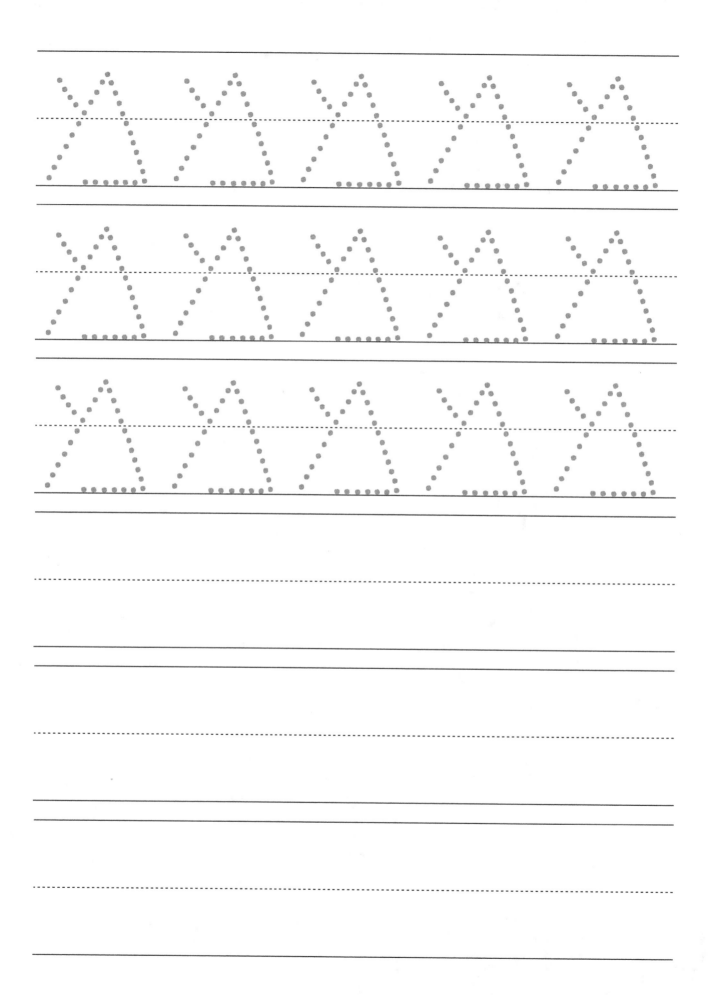

ㄅㄟㄋㄩ

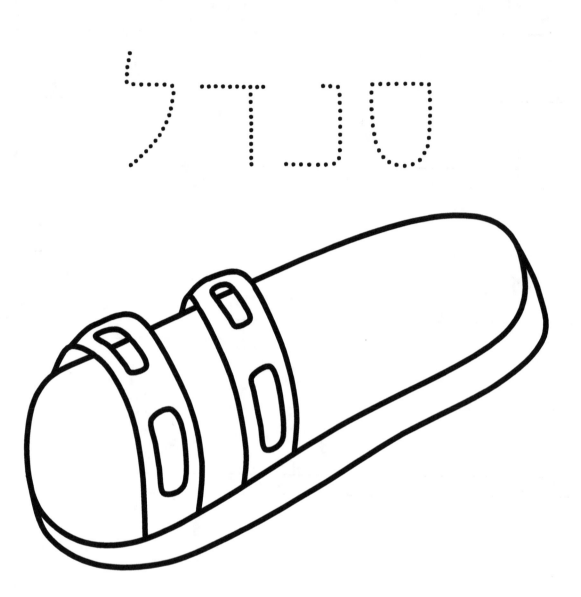

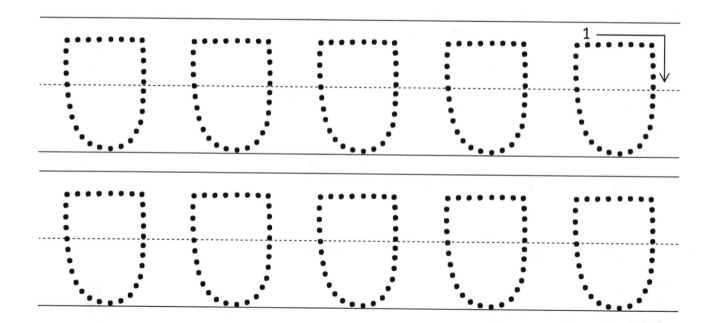

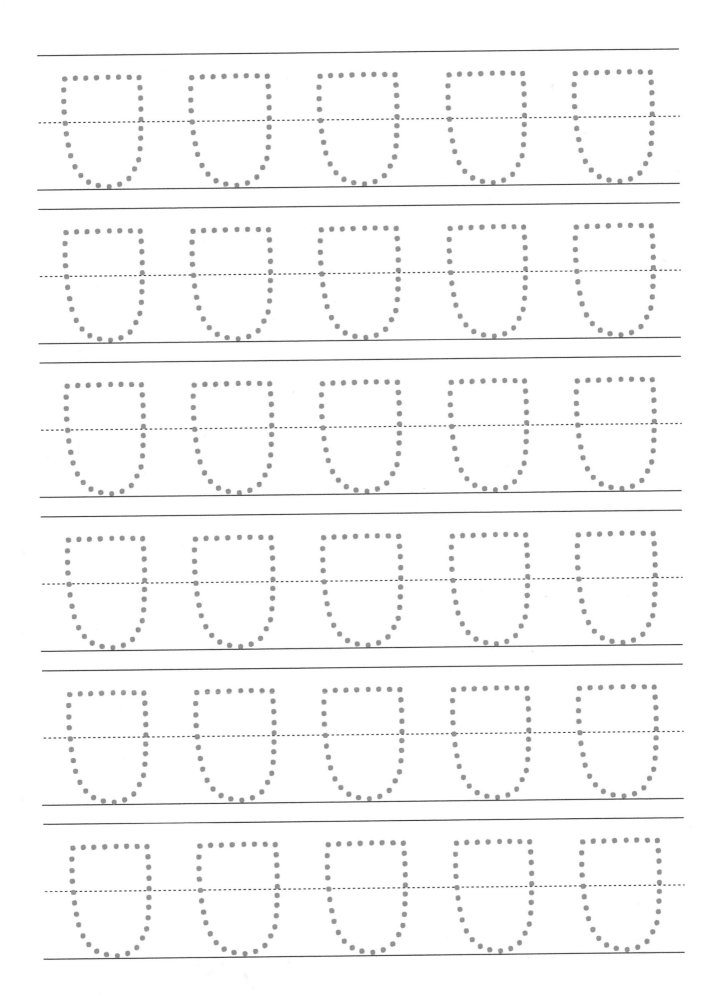

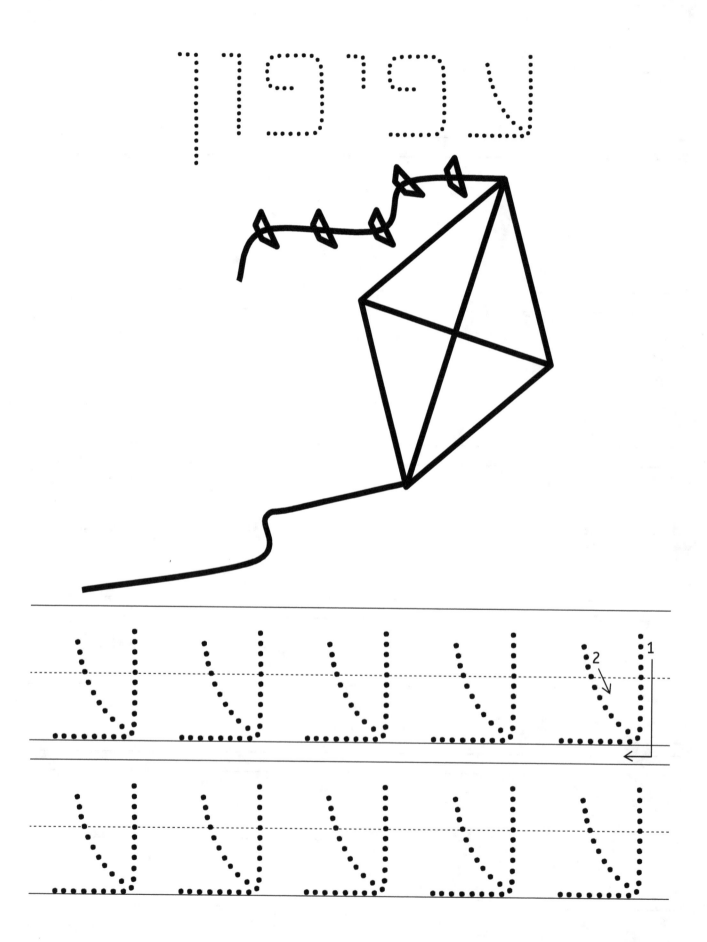

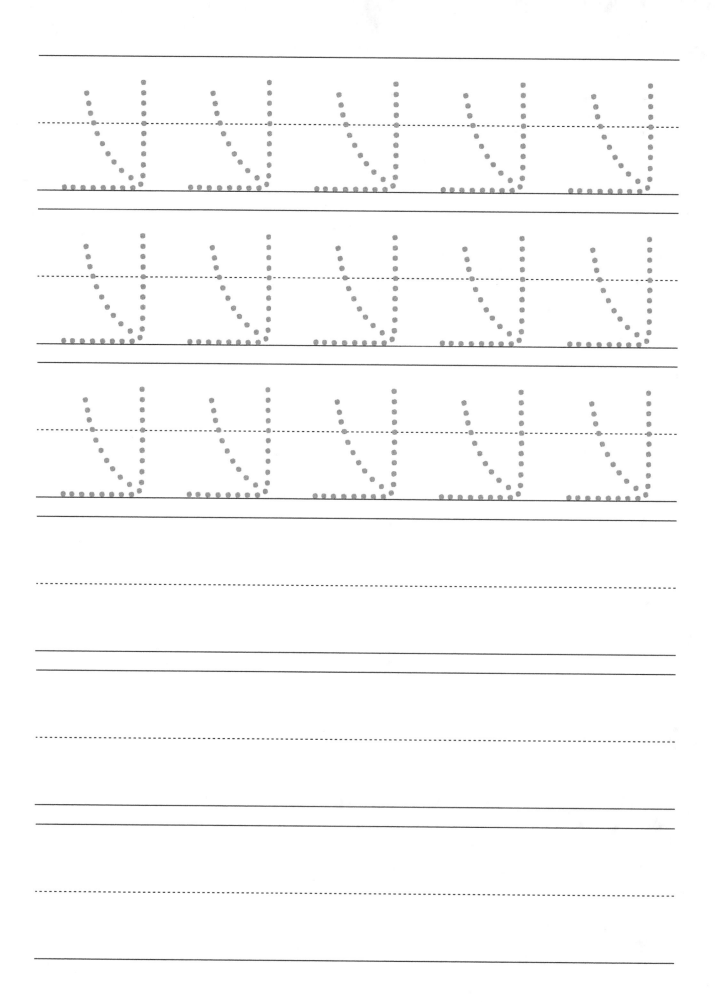

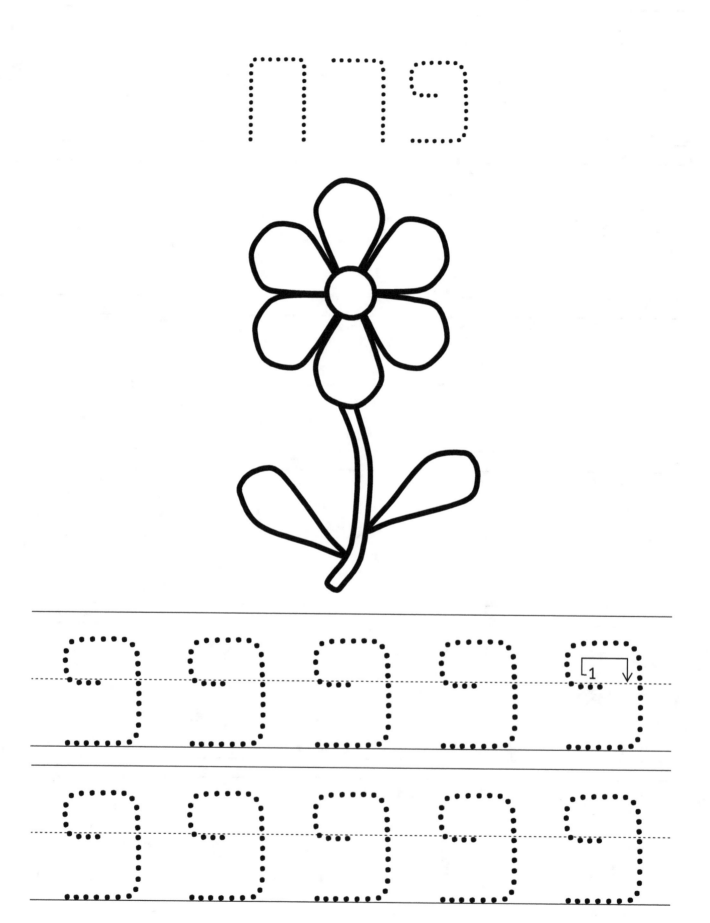

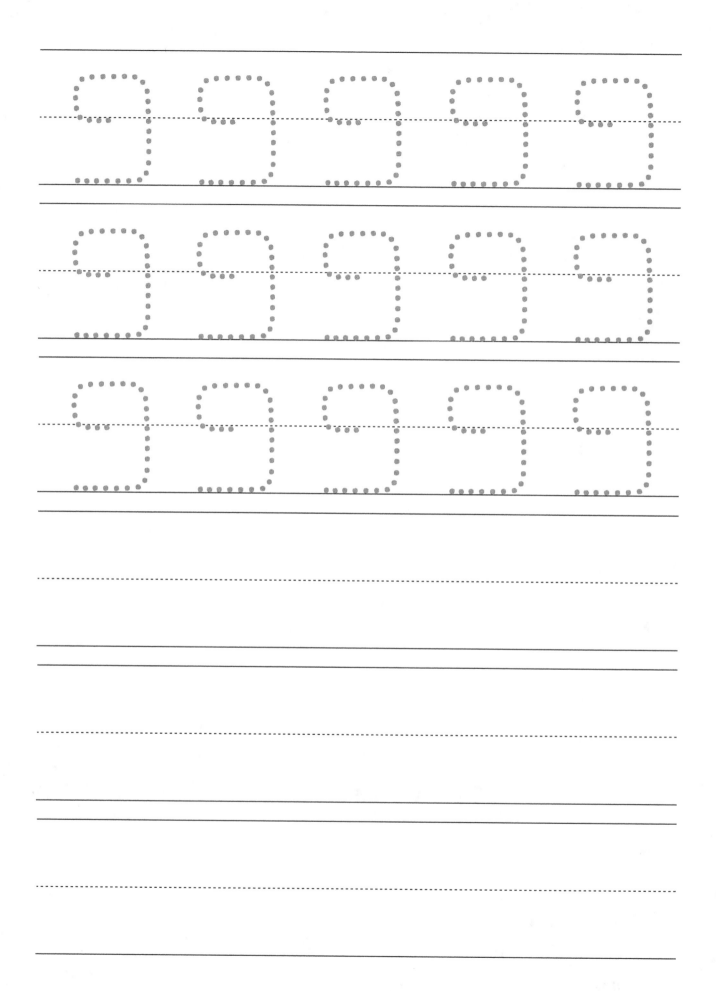

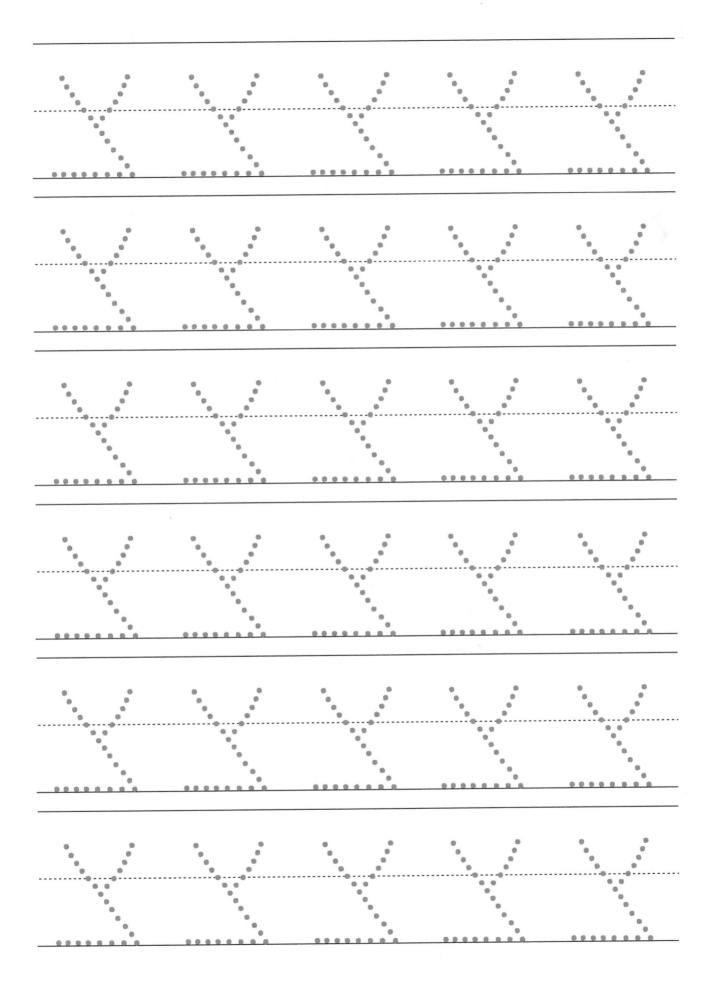

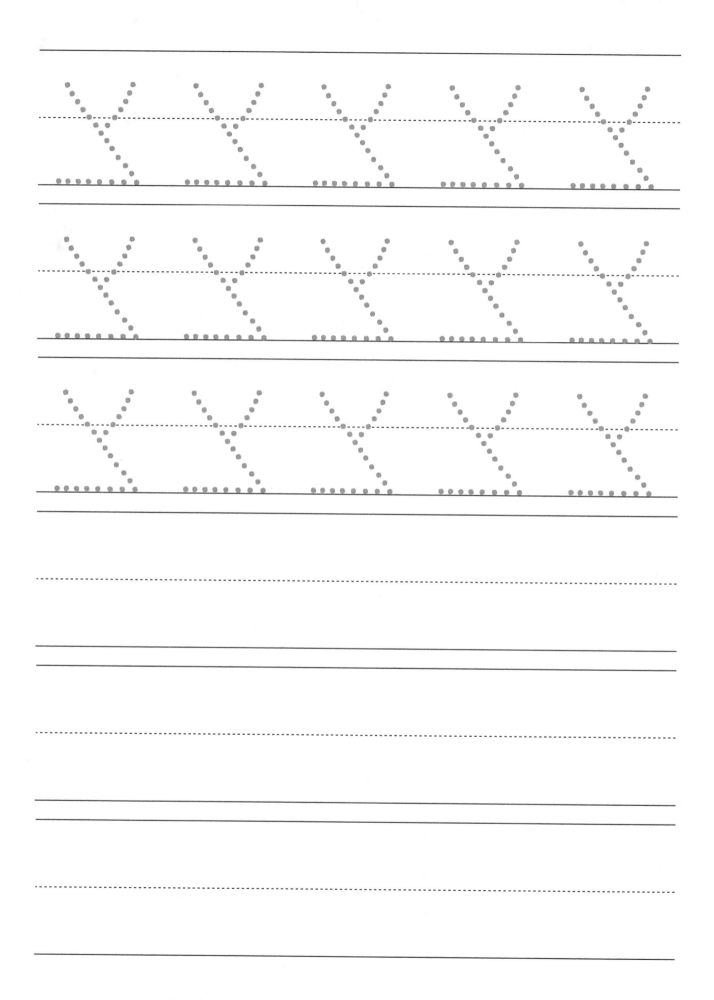

קסילופון

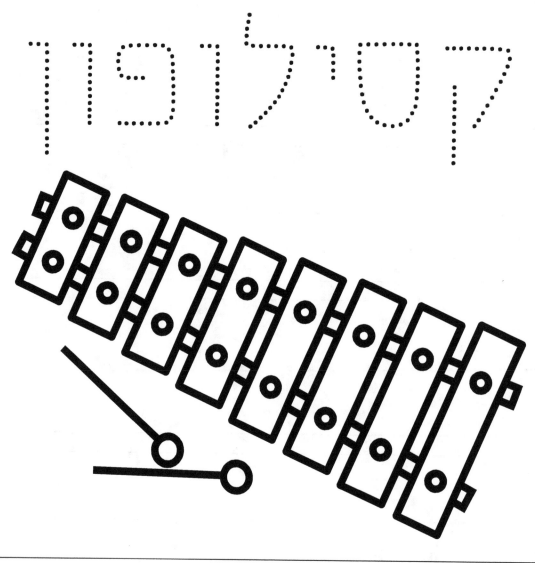

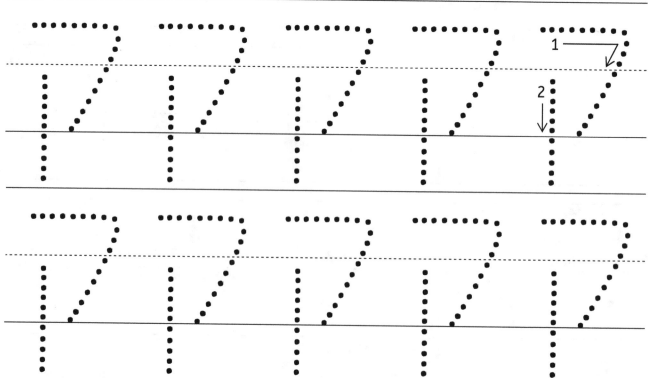

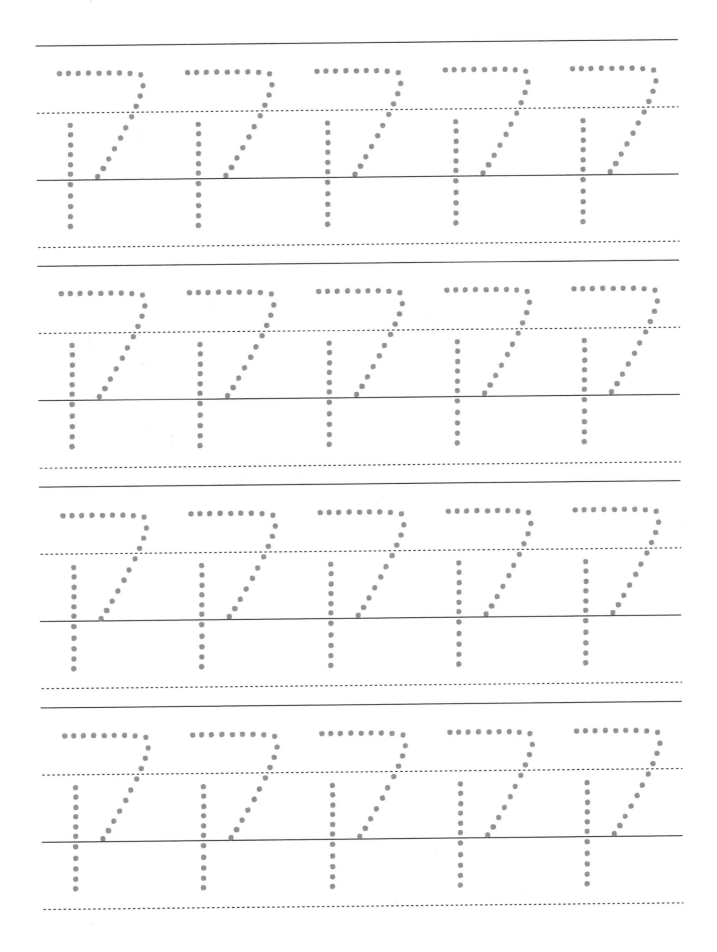

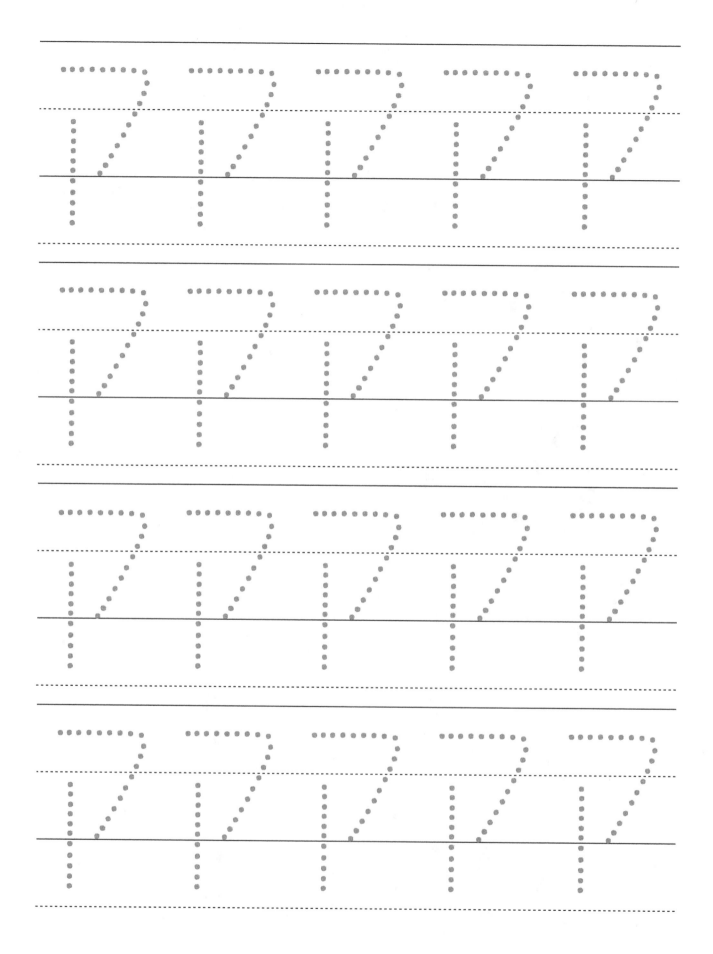

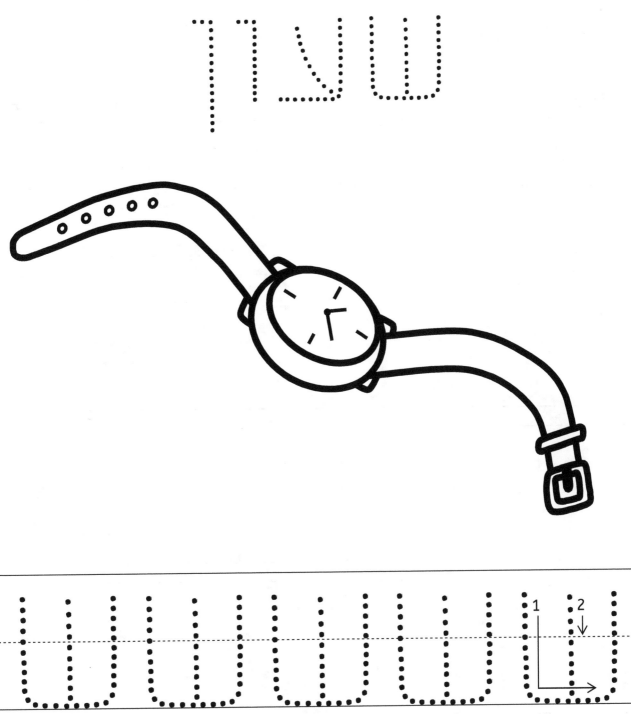

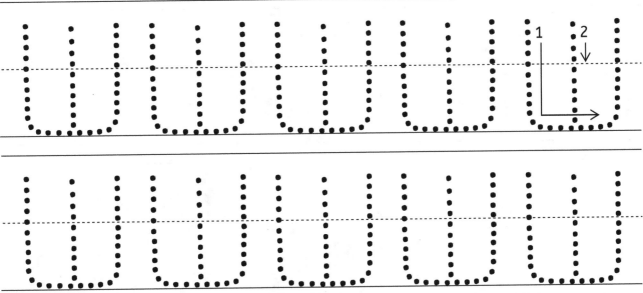

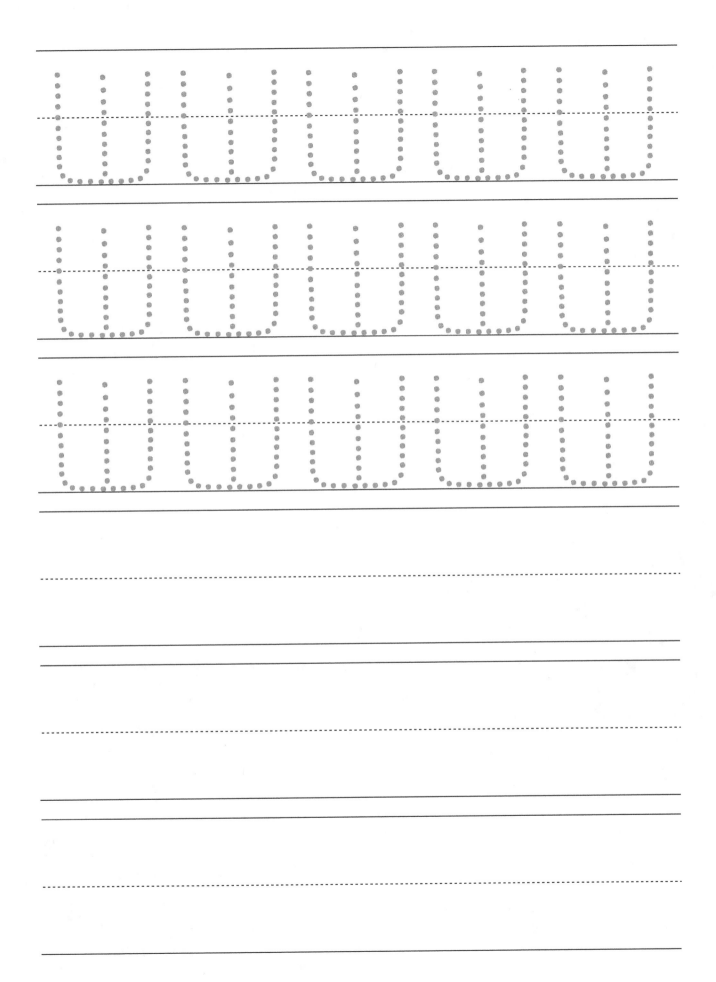

תַּפּוּחַ

2 1

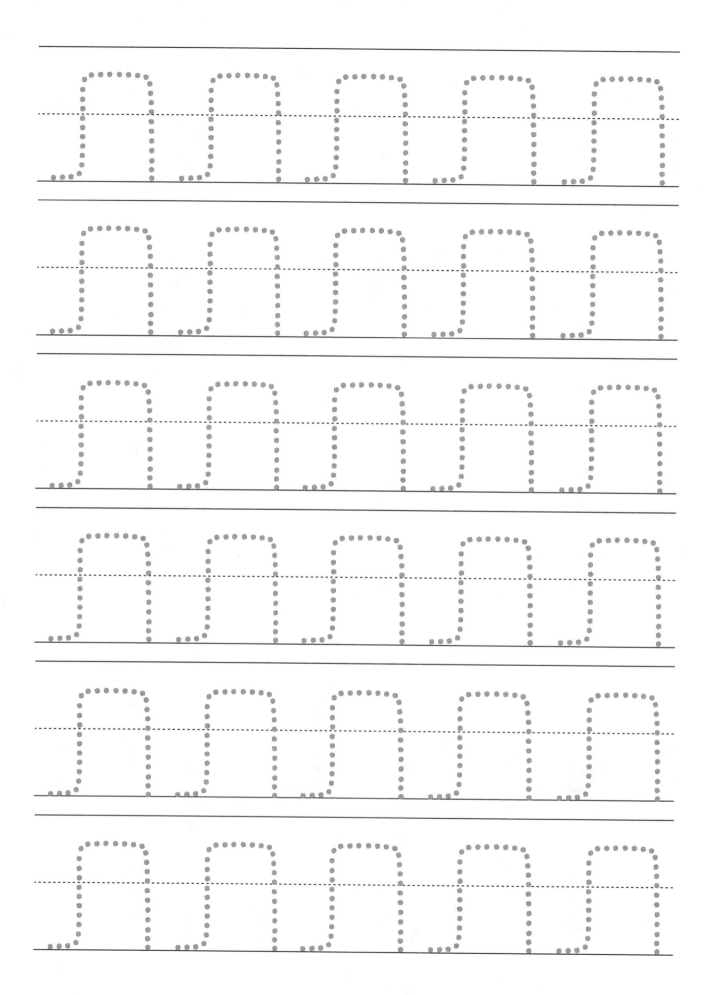

משקפיים

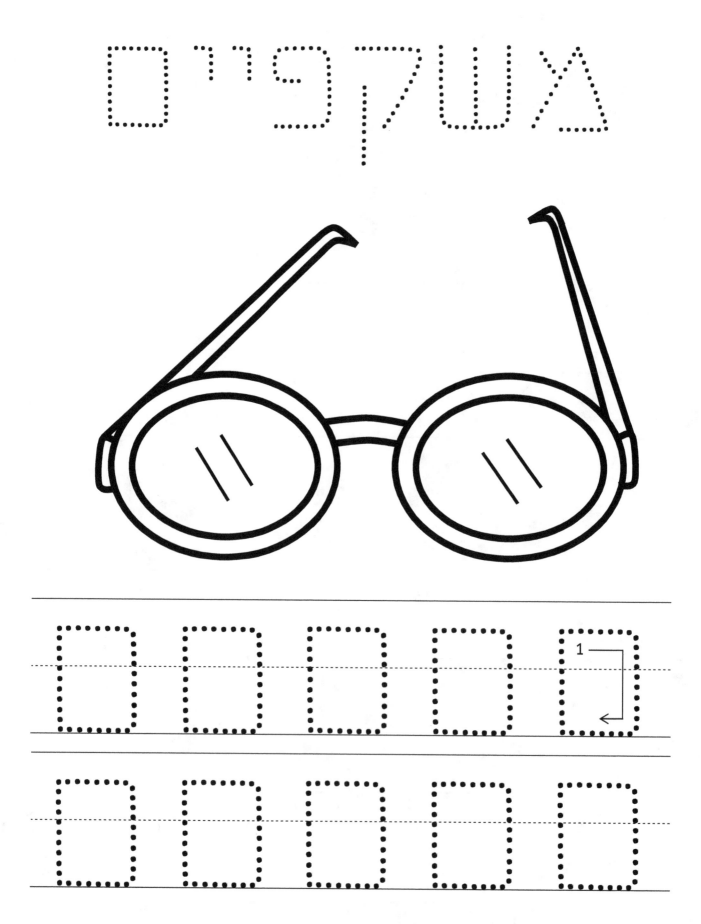

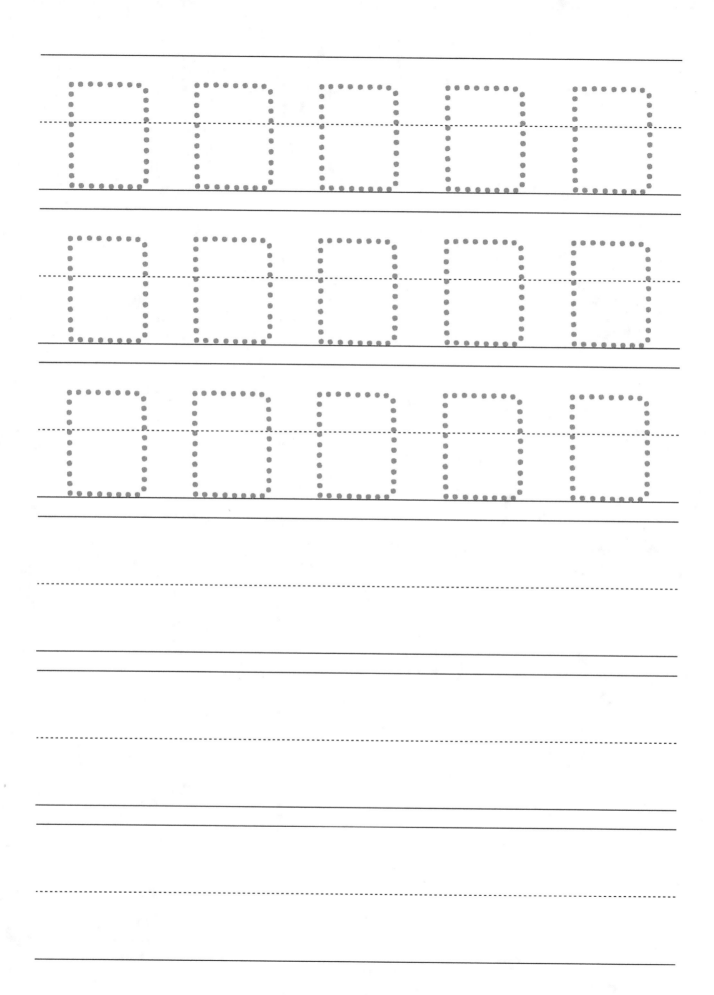

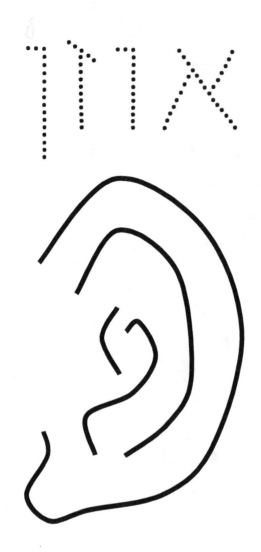

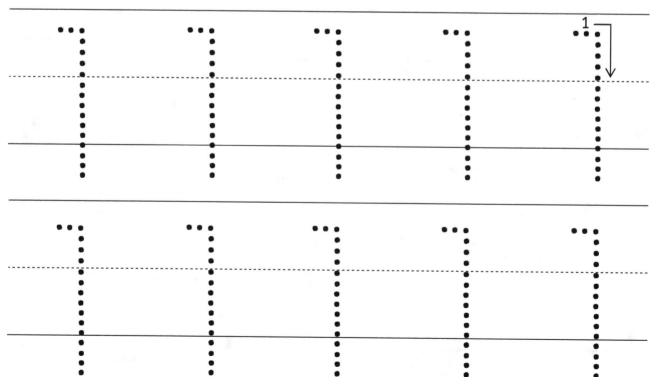

יְשׁוּף

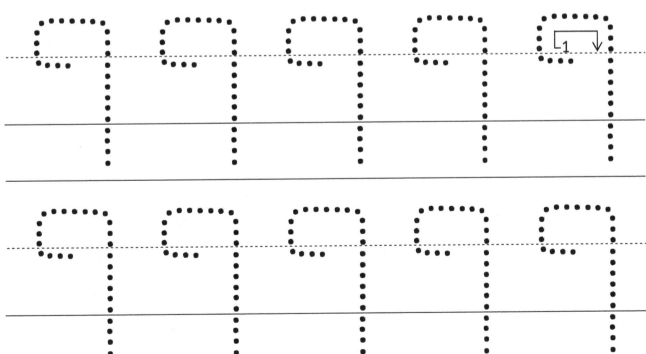

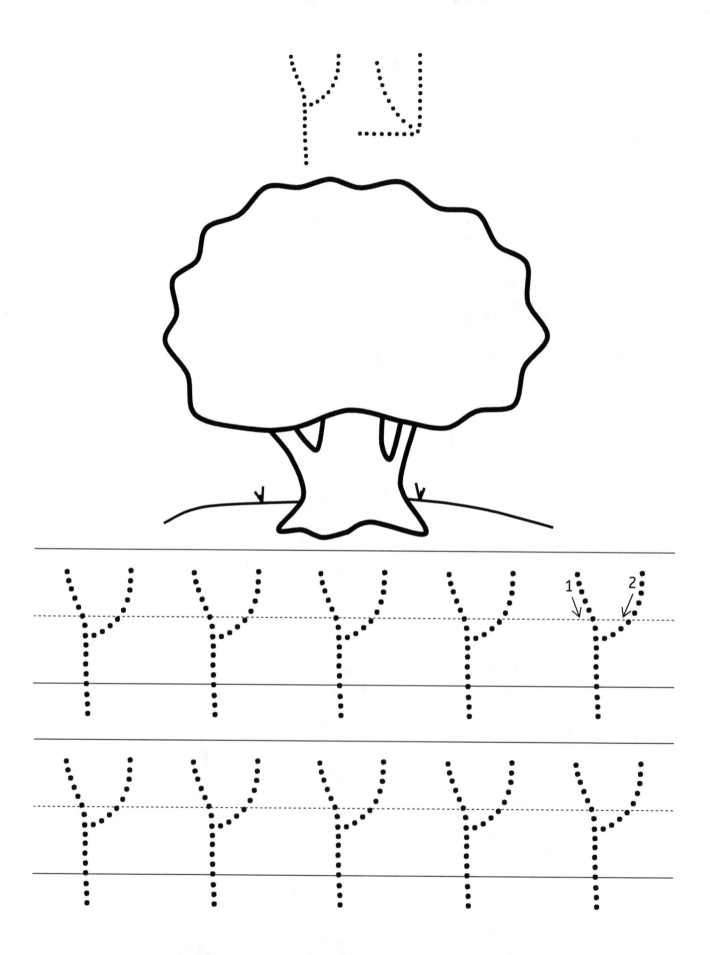

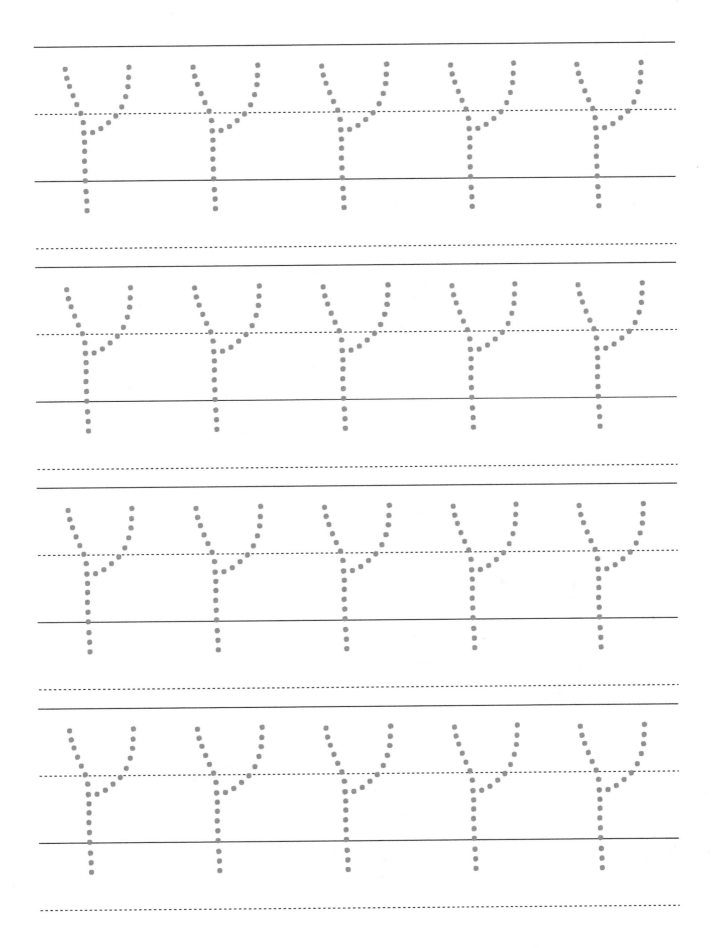

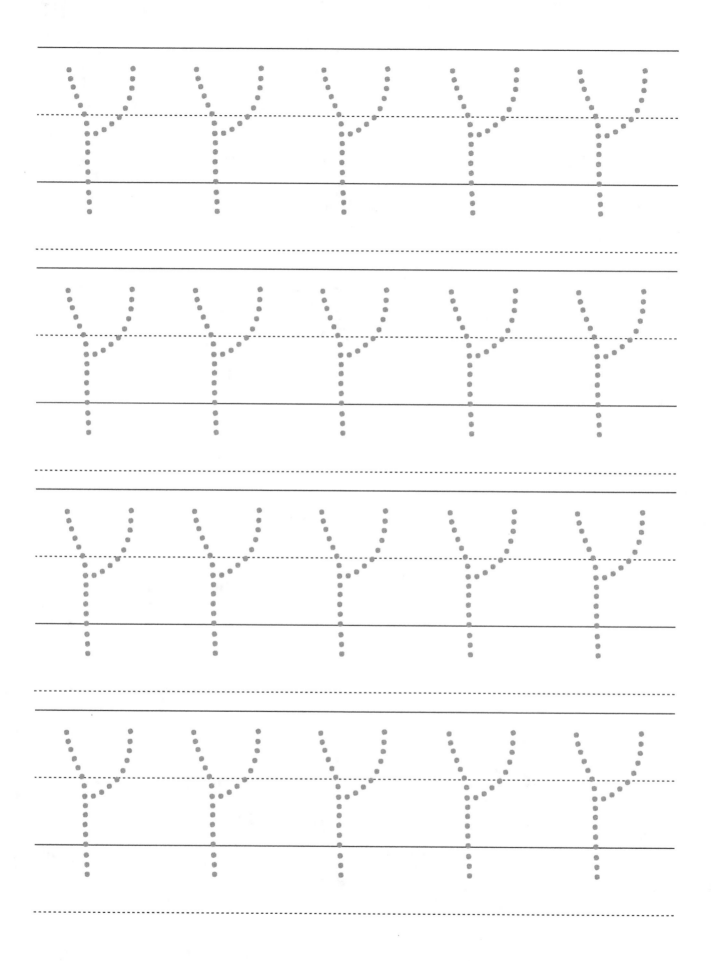

Also by Sharon Asher

Alef Bet
Tracing and Practice
Script

Hebrew
Coloring Book

אבטיח

Color the Alef Bet

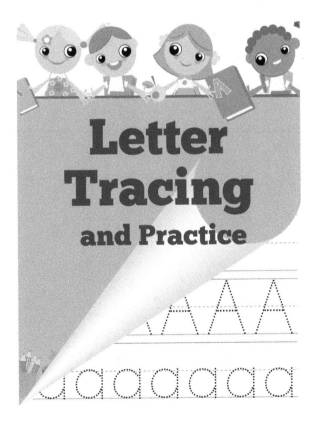

Letter Tracing
and Practice

Shape Tracing
and Practice